D1523544

DAD SHIT

A Step-by-Step Guide to Becoming a Good (Enough)
Father

Charles Moore

You're reading a humorous book by a non-expert. The lawyers say I have to include the statement below, but come on, you already know you need to be responsible for your own choices.

Neither the publisher nor the author is engaged in rendering professional advice or services to the individual reader. The ideas, procedures, and suggestions contained in this book are not intended as a substitute for consulting with a medical provider. Neither the author nor the publisher shall be liable for any loss or damage allegedly arising from any information or suggestion in this book.

Dedicated to my wife, Erin, who thought I wasn't
paying attention to all the parenting books.
Turns out I was!

To my kids, this is also dedicated to you. Sorry
for being the most mediocre father of all time.

CONTENTS

INTRODUCTION

Are you expecting your first kid? Congrats! You've just signed up for the best job ever.

One catch: Your new boss knows nothing, has zero control over their bladder, and does not give a fuuuuuuck about your feelings.

Luckily, you have a few things going for you. First, you're only legally obligated to do 18 years of this parenting thing. Fatherhood may feel like prison, but my friend Dan once said about having kids, "Sure, you lose your freedom, but you gain....what's the opposite of 'freedom' that's still good?"

Even Martha Stewart made it through her sentence in jail. You'll be fine.

Second, there's an almost 0% chance that you'll be the worst father ever. People have successfully raised kids for thousands of years, and most were much less capable than you. For instance, most people couldn't read throughout human history, and you're proving your literacy skills right now.

Most newborns only have a few needs: to eat, sleep, pee, poop, and be held. It's almost always about only one of those things when they're crying. No Ph.D. in Physics is required— you already have the tools to handle everything.

My experience is that parenting is way easier than we make it out to be ahead of time. Well, it's easy like running a marathon is easy. You just start, and if you don't stop, you'll eventually finish. You may have sore nipples and be dehydrated, but you can get to the finish line.

The most important caveat is that trying to "win" at parenting is a recipe for flaming out at mile 20 or having to crawl the last few feet. When you see the guy next to you taking off in a sprint, you have to think, "He's a fool," rather than "I can't let myself get behind." If you sprint or compare yourself to others, the race will be much more difficult for you than it has to be.

The sleep deprivation that comes with having a newborn is hard. But if you're pacing yourself instead of trying to do everything, you can get more than enough sleep over time.

Maintaining your relationship with your partner can also be difficult. But the fundamentals of what it takes to maintain a strong relationship with your partner don't change that much—you're still the same people.

Once your kid has feelings—basically, years one to 18—things get tricky. But by the time your kid throws tantrums, you will either know what you're doing or you'll have built up enough resistance to blissfully ignore their piercing meltdowns.

HI, I'M CHARLES

My wife, Erin, and I have two kids. As of writing this book, my oldest, Zola, is seven years old, and she's the greatest. My youngest kid, Charles—we call him Big Time—is five years old. He's an idiot, which is to say he's a boy.

Having two kids is helpful because it enables a comparison between the two parenting experiences. With our first kid, I was focused on being a good father. With our second, I've gained some wisdom—and I'm just trying to be *good enough*. I read books to Zola nearly every day, but I don't remember reading a single book to Big Time. Zola had a legitimate crib. Big Time slept in a Pack 'n Play. Zola needed to be held every night to fall asleep. I wouldn't have done that for Big Time, even if he cried for it. ("Man up, baby!")

Despite the significant differences in how much attention,

effort, and money my wife and I have spent on our kids, I'm happy to report that the results are about the same. Both kids are healthy, happy, and on a perfectly reasonable development trajectory. My insight from that experience is that many things we stressed about when the kids were younger were not that important for their well-being. The point of this book is to help you benefit from those parenting lessons.

For context, I grew up in a suburb outside of Detroit. My mom was a math teacher, and my dad was the stern assistant principal in your high school—the one you least wanted to see if you got in trouble. (He was like that at home as well.)

Because my parents were both educators, we were a squarely middle-class family—we were never without core needs. Still, we definitely didn't have everything we could have possibly wanted as kids.

And while my parents were pro-education, they weren't *our kids will succeed at all costs* parents. As long as we got our homework done, we could spend the rest of the day doing whatever we wanted, including nothing. This was the '80s, so like DVDs and the internet, intensive parenting hadn't yet been invented.

I mention that because my kids are growing up in a very different environment. We live on Capitol Hill in Washington, DC. Our neighborhood is filled with upwardly mobile parents who have succeeded in the rat race and seem ready to invest whatever it takes for their kids to do the same. I know people who send two-year-olds to soccer class. You read that right. It's not "come play in the park with soccer balls." It's a *class*.

My wife had our kids attend a music class—basically, a musically-inclined young adult sings and plays rhythms for a group of kids. The class is purchased as a "semester," as if it's some required educational experience to set your kid up for success.

I'm not arguing that those activities are useless—your kid

will likely have fun and learn something—but those activities are signs of a larger culture that tells us to spend more money, to worry that we're not good parents, and to be more stressed about our kid falling behind in life because Timmy down the block is already doing *advanced* story time at the local library.

That's ridiculous, and I think there's a better way to approach parenthood.

WHAT YOU'RE GOING TO GET IN THIS BOOK

You're probably reading this because you haven't read all the other new parent books yet. Having read most of them, I can tell you that there's a lot of content you don't need. Some read like a three-hour lecture on how to tie your shoes.

What you'll get here are the essentials—just enough knowledge to avoid messing things up. You only need the essentials right now because you will have Google, Amazon, and your pediatrician to help you figure things out as you go.

This is an "advice book" in that it shares a clear perspective on parenting, but I'm not here to direct your life. Instead, my goal is to help you feel confident that you know what you're doing and, tactically, to avoid the numerous mistakes I and other new fathers have made.

In addition to my direct experience as a father, I've synthesized the best material from leading new parent books. I have also enlisted The Distinguished Council of Dads to share their experiences in this book. They're really just a bunch of good friends—though they're all accomplished and cool dudes in their own right. You'll see their perspectives throughout.

Finally, this is a two-beer book—it's designed for you to complete it in the time it takes you to drink a couple of brews. If it takes longer than that, you're probably drinking too fast. Sober up, and it'll be a fast read.

WHAT "GOOD ENOUGH" GETS YOU: A COMPARISON

GOOD FATHER	GOOD ENOUGH FATHER
Reading 10 boring children's books to your newborn every day	Reading ESPN articles to them because words are words and stories are stories
Even one second of screen time is bad	Maybe just don't have the TV on all day
Buying the best gear for the kid	Buying whatever makes **your** life easier
"We will fail if they don't get into Harvard or Yale or Stanford."	"As long as they can read and know how to work hard, that's fine."
Stressing about everything	Focusing on what really matters and relaxing about everything else

GEARING UP

I wish I had known how much time I would spend in the aisles of the pharmacy during years 1-3. The amount of children's medicine and diapers purchased was unbelievable.

———

Ken

My good friend Mason is a competent business professional, but if you talked to him for more than five minutes, you would learn that he is a super fan of fried chicken. Having tried roughly 96% of the restaurants that offer fried chicken in the Washington, DC metro area, Mason has a sommelier-level understanding of it. Based on his belief in great flavor and disdain for overspending— "Fried chicken's return on flavor (ROF) plateaus after $20"—Mason's favorite place is a hole-in-the-wall in our neighborhood called H&Chicken. Whenever we're at a party together, there's a 93% chance the conversation eventually lands on, "Are we going to order H&Chicken on the way home?"

Beyond his deep knowledge of fried chicken, Mason is also an expert in rapidly gearing up to have a baby. He gained that expertise because his first kid, Gordon, arrived weeks early—importantly, two days before the baby shower at which Mason and his wife Rosemary would have received all of the gear they needed.

When they had to rush to the hospital for the birth, Mason and his wife had nothing ready—no crib, car seat, or clothes. I imagine getting the call that his wife was in labor was like hearing a fire alarm when you're in the shower. You've got to go outside with your cheeks out whether you like it or not.

Despite being unprepared, Mason and his wife had two critical things in their possession: (a) friends and (b) an Amazon account. My wife and I helped them track down a car seat from a family who had just outgrown it. Other friends did a grocery store run to stock their refrigerator and sourced a few onesies. Mason and Rosemary ordered the rest of what they needed from Amazon. By the time they came home from the hospital, they had everything they needed.

The lesson is that wherever you are in your preparation, you'll be fine.

YOU CAN BUY WAY LESS THAN YOU THINK

Parenting is about cleaning. At any given moment, your newborn will either be spitting up on their clothes or having poop so explosive that the diaper can't handle it. Since you'll be doing laundry every five minutes, having a week's worth of clothing options is unnecessary. (Also, everyone else will buy your kid clothes, so you don't have to.) It's the same for bottles. You will have to clean the bottles immediately after use to avoid bacteria growth, so you can get by with only having a few of them.

Overall, having a kid is a never-ending battle with having too much shit. At one point, my daughter Zola had 15 stuffed animals—all gifts given to her. She played with maybe two of them. She has at least ten pairs of shoes, even though she only prefers one at a time. We have what seems like 3,000 books, but the kids read the same ten books at any given time. The list goes on.

So start with less, and stay vigilant.

You can also get away with buying less as long as Amazon ships to you within two days or you live less than ten minutes from a grocery store. The only things you need to have on hand at all times are diapers, wipes, and allergy medicine—everything else you can buy when you need it.

The other benefit of keeping a low stock of gear and supplies is that it gives you an excuse to take a break from parenting. "We need some paper towels? I'll take care of it, honey. Be back in three hours."

I'm kidding about the three hours, but if you're like me, taking a few minutes for a mental break without anyone crying or talking to you will be pretty clutch in the chaotic early days.

Besides—and this may sound sad—going to the grocery store may be the most fun thing you do all day when you have a newborn. I remember strolling down each aisle of the store to squeeze just a little bit more out of the trip.

GET ALL THE USED GEAR YOU CAN

Almost anything you can buy used should be perfectly fine.

Because we were wiser with our second kid, we bought nothing for Big Time's arrival. That meant, for example, that he would sometimes wear hot pink onesies with bows on them. That challenged my outdated notions of gender, but he didn't care how fashionable his clothes were or whether someone else had previously worn them. All babies care about is whether they are warm enough.

Buying used gear and voraciously seeking hand-me-downs is a great way to save money, especially on things like the baby's car seat or stroller, which can cost hundreds. And if you're worried about safety, know that 99.9% of baby stuff is plastic. If it doesn't biodegrade in a dump in 1,000 years, it'll undoubtedly be fine after a year of another kid using it. (The only thing that makes a used car seat hazardous is if it's been in a significant accident. As long as you trust the person offering it, it's all good.)

Beyond the financial savings, most of your parent friends actually want to get rid of their accumulated baby gear. You're doing them a favor by taking their hand-me-downs. Just ask.

Then again, if you've got Bill Gates money, fuck it. Buy that diamond-encrusted pacifier.

YOUR KID DOESN'T HAVE A STYLE OR STANDARDS

When you're buying your kid new Jordans or a fresh outfit, you're doing it for yourself. They could care less. Moreover, using the "best" products will be lost entirely on your kid. It's like buying a Johnnie Walker Blue Label bottle for a man with no taste buds. As I mentioned, our second kid slept in a Pack 'n Play. But he never complained about the lack of an actual crib because he did not know what it felt like to sleep in anything else.

Mason, whose story you read earlier, shared this perspective:

> Don't buy the most top-tier gear that money can buy. It doesn't have any more utility than the Toyota-level equivalent. I like the UPPAbaby stroller, but was it twice the utility of a $500 one? The jury is still out. But since all my friends have it, it's given us admission into the bourgeois stroller gang.

So yeah, if you're trying to impress your rich friends or look good to your Instagram followers, buy your kid a bunch of fancy stuff.

Just don't pretend it's for your kid's benefit.

JUST BECAUSE IT SAYS "BABY" DOESN'T MEAN IT'S BETTER

America's marketers seem to have figured out they can charge a premium when they slap the word *baby* on something. The most egregious instance of this I've seen is "baby purified water."

What is "baby purified water," you ask? It's plain water.

As you start to gear up, realize that a product's claim to be for babies often means little about whether it's better for your kid or more useful to you. Here are some examples of baby-labeled items that fall into this category:

- Diaper bag—you can use any old backpack instead.

- Bottle drying rack—just use any kind of dish rack or drying pad. Separating your baby tools from your other dishes is helpful, but you don't need a special-purpose item.

- Baby towels—the towels you already own are fine.

- Baby lotion—any gentle, unscented lotion will do.

It's not that these baby-labeled items aren't marginally more helpful. It's that you can save money and space by not buying them. And you can stick it to our capitalist overlords in the process.

A COUNCIL OF DADS BUYING GUIDE

I asked the Council of Dads for their thoughts on what items they found useless and what they thought was most helpful. Here are some of the best answers.

THINGS YOU DON'T NEED

- Wipe warmers—"Such a waste."

- Bottle sanitizers—"You can use boiling water or, you know, soap."

- Baby cookbooks—"I didn't have time to cook for myself, much less the baby."

- Toys—"People will buy toys for my kids forever, even if I don't want or need them." "Don't underestimate the value of allowing their creativity to identify and create toys (behold the power of a fallen branch!)."

- Educational apps—"There is a ton of good and free content available."

I see several themes in those answers. If you'd have to completely change your lifestyle to use it (e.g., a baby cookbook for someone who doesn't cook), it's probably not worth it. If there's a reasonable free substitute, try that first. And if others will buy it for you, save your money.

TOTALLY WORTH IT

- "Anything that makes [the baby's] sleeping easier."

- "A house with a spare bedroom so parents/in-laws can stay long term to help take care of the kiddo."

- "Getting a Costco card is clutch so you can buy 48 bottles of baby smoothies at once."

- "Jogging stroller. Helped fight the dad bod."

- "A vacation?"

Someone also recommended getting a minivan. But I refuse to co-sign that weak idea. As an experienced dad told me, "You can either buy a car that fits that huge stroller, or you can just buy a smaller stroller that fits the car you really want."

I fully endorse that idea. You'll make a lot of sacrifices for your kid—buying a minivan doesn't need to be one of them.

For me, the most valuable items for parenting were only loosely related to the kids. Instead, they were the things that made my wife and me more comfortable. For example:

- A new iPad and headphones for a better binge-watching experience while rocking my kid back to sleep

- A bottle of very good scotch to loosen up after a hard day of parenting

- A knee pad to help when kneeling over the tub during

bathtime

Your kid hasn't done anything in life. They've never put in a shift at a job they can barely stand so they can provide for their family. They've never even cleaned their own ass after a massive deuce. They don't deserve the brand-new, luxury gear.

You do.

Treat yourself.

HAVING THE CONVERSATION WITH YOUR PARTNER

I stand behind everything said here and suspect that you'll fully agree once you have experience as a father. But it's worth acknowledging that this advice may counter your instincts.

You and your partner may be thinking more about the peace of mind that comes from having everything you might possibly need or the satisfaction of giving your kid "the best." Those are very legitimate motivations. Again, you gotta do you.

And even if you are on board with these approaches, getting your partner on board may be challenging. So unless buying all the gear is breaking your budget, it may not be worth starting an argument. A refrain you will see throughout this book: It's not worth getting divorced.

If you want a gentler, more practical approach, enlist experienced parent friends to help make the case for constrained buying. For example, you might suggest, "Before we go out and buy anything, how about we ask [list a few people who you know your partner trusts] what they found more or less useful?"

That way, you'll change the conversation from "my view" versus "your view" to something more productive.

GETTING READY

Set your expectations for difficulty level: hardcore. That way, it'll always be easier since you're over-prepared.

Mason

PREGNANCY, A BRIEF TIMELINE

SEX
~ 40 weeks out

You didn't win the Sex Olympics, but you got the job done.

SHE'S F-ING OVER IT
4-6 weeks before the due

This is the *painfully pregnant* phase. Your wife will be done with the whole damn experiment.

GET READY, STAY
3 weeks before the due date

The baby is officially at term. The kid probably won't come this early, but don't be surprised.

THE DUE DATE

THE REAL DUE DATE
8 days later

Despite what the doctor told you and what you've been telling everyone else, first babies come, on average, eight days after the due date. Confusing, but yeah.

YOU FINALLY HAVE YOUR SHIT TOGETHER
like 18 years later

Fake it until you make it.

O bviously, your partner has **by far** the most work to do during pregnancy. This chapter will help you prepare for everything else—preparing your finances, naming the baby, and packing for the hospital.

START GETTING READY EARLY

Do yourself a favor and banish the concept of a "due date" from your head.

First, it's misleading. As Emily Oster writes in *Expecting Better*, "[W]ithout any intervention, the average woman pregnant with her first child goes into labor a full 8 days after her supposed 'due date.'"[1] And despite the average birth happening after the supposed due date, the reasonable window for your baby to be born starts several weeks before.

Second, the distribution curve of births around the due date looks like a speed bump, not a mountain. About a week before my first kid was born, I looked up the data on births in the U.S.—partly because I was nervous and partly because I'm a nerd. That data shows that the actual likelihood of the birth happening on any single day is relatively low. If it's your due date, and you're thinking, "Today's the day," you're most likely wrong.

So be ready, but relax.

That said, there are two things you should tackle ASAP if you have not done so already:

1. Buy and install the car seat—they won't let you leave the hospital without it.

2. Put your personal hospital bag in the car. You want it with you rather than at the house because you may have to meet your wife at the hospital if she goes into labor when you're not with her.

There's no reason you couldn't crush those two tasks—like right now.

GETTING READY TO SPEND MONEY

Even if you have health insurance, the average person pays over $2,800 out of pocket for pregnancy, childbirth, and postpartum care expenses.[2] If your employer-provided health plan's annual coverage election is coming up, you might investigate whether the higher tier plans may save you money or consider putting more in a Health Savings Account so you can pay for the medical care with pre-tax money.

The hospital will bill your insurance for your partner's care, but they will bill you directly for the baby's care. Hence, it is worth checking with your health insurer to see if you can add your new kid to the plan before birth, potentially saving you the hassle of submitting billing paperwork later. (Either way, most employer plans enable you to add a kid and adjust your insurance coverage options right after they are born.)

You may have an older family member who seems to always have a recently purchased luxury car or is on vacation as if they have money to burn and no cares in the world. Those are the people who never had kids. In my family, that's my wife's cousin, Everett. They call him Big Money.

I still remember the day I told my wife what having our first kid would do to our household budget. We were out for brunch while she was pregnant. I said, "With the new house and after we start paying for childcare, we'll be break-even each month." You should have seen the stunned look on her face. We wouldn't be broke, but our days of going to fancy restaurants without thinking too much about the cost were numbered.

One day, when my daughter was an infant, she fell asleep during a car ride. Since I had an hour to kill, I decided to visit a nearby Porsche dealership on the way home just to check out the new models—you know, as guys do. But the very second I walked into the showroom, Zola woke up and started crying loudly. It was like she was intent on yelling to everyone, "MY DAD CANNOT AFFORD ANYTHING HERE!"

Without understanding the concept of money, she'd somehow figured out her impact on the family finances.

The important thing to understand about the impact of kids on your budget is that it's mostly the infrastructure for the kid that matters, not what the kid consumes. According to the U.S. government, housing is the most expensive part of raising a kid.[3] For my family, that was moving from a one-bedroom apartment to a three-bedroom house. Though the house is likely an excellent long-term investment, it created a massively higher monthly cash outflow.

Another big expense category is transportation.[4] If you already have a car, you'll be fine. You don't need to upgrade to a minivan for just one kid. But my family went from a "downtown with no car" lifestyle to a "residential neighborhood with two cars" lifestyle. Seemingly overnight, we went from spending $0 on cars to having two monthly car payments.

Even if you have the house and car situation settled, childcare expenses will make you weep. Childcare is expensive because you're paying human beings to keep your kid alive. There are no efficiencies in that business. The actual cost will depend on what type of care you choose and where you live, but it will surely body-slam your wallet like The Rock in his prime.

Almost everything else is a rounding error compared to the house, car, and childcare expenses. When kids are young, they're either on breastmilk, which is free, or formula, which costs just a few bucks a day. Diapers are also only a few bucks a day.

ESTATE PLANNING: GET ON IT

Get life insurance.

Create a will.

If there's one place in this book where I'll be dogmatic, it's here. Your role as a father is to protect your family. If you don't have an estate plan, you're not doing fatherhood right.

You don't necessarily need anything fancy—if something happened to you, you'd most likely leave everything to your partner—so don't let the perfect be the enemy of the good. Just get it done. Your kid is relying on you.

DON'T GET DIVORCED OVER NAMING THE BABY

Since my father and grandfather are both named Charles, my wife and I had previously agreed—almost as a prenuptial agreement—that our son's first name would be Charles. Regardless of the family legacy, it is objectively the best name anyone could have.

Once we found out we were having a girl, we started tossing out names to each other. The problem, however, was that we would also instantly judge each other's suggestions.

"How about Thelma?"

"That name is stupid."

"That's my grandmother's name."

I hated that dynamic. It wasn't great for our marital bliss to shoot down each other's ideas like we were in an epic round of *Call of Duty*.

What made it worse was that my wife and I were making those judgments based on criteria we had yet to really think through. Things like: "I know someone with that name, and I don't like them," or "I used to hook up with someone with that name." ("Oh, you did? Tell me more. I want to hear all about her.")

So, to create a more productive dynamic, we devised another approach. Below is a description of what we did. It may be overkill for you, but it helped us create a less judgment- and conflict-filled process.

STEP 1. SET CRITERIA

We first identified "screens" or reasons we wouldn't consider a name. For example, we would not consider names that were difficult to spell or would produce a sing-songy effect when paired with our last name (e.g., Lenore Moore). Working together, we identified "plus factors," like family names and the names of people we would like the kid to look up to, and "minus factors," like names that were faddish or too popular.

This approach was successful because we did those steps *before* looking at specific names. It forced us to clarify what was in our minds and enabled us to understand better what the other person was thinking.

STEP 2. SET A NOMINATION PERIOD

We gave ourselves three weeks to come up with ideas. During that nomination period, however, we specifically avoided sharing the names with each other to avoid making premature judgments.

(Pro Tip: If you set a limit of 10 or 15 ideas each, there's less work to do later.)

STEP 3. APPLY THE SCREENS AND RATE THE NAMES

Once we had the list of names, we created a survey that
asked us to put each name into one of the following
categories: Top 5, Second 5, Third 5, and The Rest.

Unlike our verbal interactions on naming, the survey was
designed to avoid conflict by not having an "I don't like this"
option. If you did not like a name, it simply did not make
your top 15. Second, the survey steered away from a forced
ranking (e.g., 1, 2, 3, 4, 5...) of the ideas because declaring
our favorite name might make us less open to other options
and make the subsequent discussions more contentious.
Because I'm a nerd, there was also a scoring algorithm to
add the plus and minus factors to our survey results.

The major benefit of that approach is that, by definition, the
names that rose to the top were ones we *both* liked, and we
could get to a smaller list of options quickly. That made the
rest of the naming conversation, which proceeded as you'd
expect, much easier. And eventually, one name sounded just
right.

BABY NAMING MATH

The name of your favorite grandmother who cared for you when times were tough **=** Your wife's childhood enemy, stemming from a playground incident in elementary school

Your wife's favorite singer's name **=** A woman you dated right before meeting her

(Beyoncé, you broke my heart!)

Your actual name, which you share with your father, grandfather, and great grandfather **=** "Truth be told, I've never really liked your name. Besides, it's not a good name for a baby."

Whatever name you ultimately select, there is a 100% chance it's the exact name of a porn star, convicted felon, or alt-right activist.

(*never* Google the name)

PACK LIKE NO ONE CARES ABOUT YOU AT THE HOSPITAL

It's all about mom and baby at the hospital, so you have to take care of yourself. Here's how to prepare based on that fact.

SLEEP

The hospital ain't the Four Seasons—the bed won't be great.

After a horrible sleep the first night, I went home to get my own pillow. I also brought a yoga mat to put on top of the bed to even out the pressure of the coils. And that only made it *barely* tolerable. Plan for what you need.

Moreover, a near-constant stream of doctors and nurses will enter the hospital room. They aren't there to see you, so they won't keep the lights or their voices low just because you're sleeping. Pack whatever you need to handle the disruption—e.g., earplugs, eye masks, and noise-canceling headphones.

Your newborn will cry at a decibel level and mind-piercing frequency that will get through just about any level of fatigue or technology solution you might have to block sound. Unless you're using the noise-blocking headphones they give to the aircraft marshallers who direct planes to the gate, there is basically a 0% chance that you won't hear your kid cry.

STAYING WARM

I'm from Michigan, so my hometown pride dictates that I never admit to being cold. However, the hospital room temperature will likely be well below 72 degrees. The situation calls for a hoodie. If you're fancy, perhaps a cashmere sweater vest. Either way, be prepared.

STAYING AWAKE

The day Big Time was born, I tried to stop by my favorite coffee shop on the way to the hospital. I didn't think it would be a problem since we knew exactly what time we were supposed to arrive. When my wife noticed we were not on the most direct route to the hospital, she asked, "Why are you going this way?"

She was decidedly not enthused by the detour. To save the marriage, I skipped the coffee shop.

Once we arrived at the hospital, the doctor was tied up with another patient, so there was plenty of time to visit the Starbucks next door. But I should have been more prepared with my caffeine plan.

If you're the kind of coffee person who grinds your beans and spends 15 minutes making a pour-over at home, the free coffee at the hospital definitely will not meet your refined tastes. I also recommend having a ready-to-go caffeine option in your hospital bag, like a bottle of Coca-Cola. That option will be valuable if your partner goes into labor at night and you can't justify a nap, like I had, or ten minutes to get a latte.

SNACKS

Pack some.

One of the Council Members shared this: "My wife is still pissed that I (allegedly) ate half of a crappy bagel that the hospital [cafeteria] brought for her. Later, she was hungry and didn't have food to eat. I think I got clear consent for the half-bagel, but boy, I really wish I had just packed more snacks and not touched the shit the hospital brought for her."

ENTERTAINMENT

You'll be at the hospital for several days, and there's a lot of downtime. Once your kid is born, they'll spend most of their time sleeping, and your partner will be recovering. You'll need things to occupy your attention.

My push present to myself before Zola was born was a new iPad, which I specifically bought to entertain myself at the hospital. The trip home after the kid was born—the one that was ostensibly about getting the supplies I didn't realize we needed—also served as an opportunity to download new movies onto the iPad.

Since your kid will wake up often at night, you'll likely be running on little sleep while at the hospital. So, leave the dense nonfiction books at home and opt for your favorite low-mental-calorie reality TV shows.

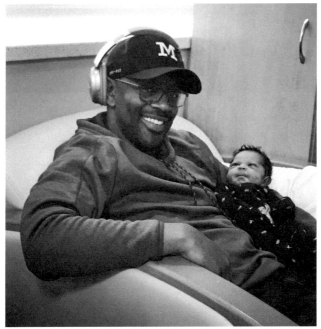

Me and Big Time at the hospital. Note the hoodie and noise-canceling headphones and the early indoctrination into Michigan fandom.

CRUSHING IT AT THE HOSPITAL

Even though it doesn't sound like [the baby is] breathing at night... they definitely are breathing, so get some sleep.

———

Dr. Shaka

This chapter assumes your significant other will give birth in a hospital. If you plan to have the birth elsewhere, skip to the next chapter. No judgment—I get that some people enjoy lukewarm milk or the middle seat on airplanes.

For everyone else, read on.

ASSUME YOUR BIRTH PLAN IS WRONG

You and your wife have a birth plan, eh? Yeah, good luck with that. Unless you're a doctor and have experienced numerous deliveries, I humbly offer you this: You don't know what the hell you're talking about.

For the birth of my first kid, my wife and I arrived at the hospital around 7:00 p.m. She was in labor, but you know, not *labor* labor. The baby wasn't going to arrive for several hours. We watched several episodes of *House of Cards*, and I eventually took a nap.

It was a disorienting experience because I had been misled by the birthing video we'd seen during the hospital tour several weeks earlier. The video depicted women enduring painful labor while walking up and down the halls and bouncing on balls to move things along. At every step, the father provided dutiful support, like offering ice and giving massages. It looked like a lot of activity, all happening over a few short daylight hours. I prepared myself for that role, and I definitely did not envision the downtime and asking the doctor questions like, "Is it ok if I take a nap?"

The video was also misleading because it only included

women who did not use the pain medicine. What I didn't understand at the time was that once my wife got an epidural (sometime the next morning), she would be stuck in bed for the rest of labor. That shift substantially decreased my (physical) role in the birth process. Mostly, I looked up from the iPad every 20 minutes and asked, "Do you need anything?"

After several more hours of labor, the doctor told us the baby wasn't "tolerating" the birth process, which meant they wanted to change the plan and do a cesarean section to reduce the risk of complications. In hindsight, they had signaled the possibility hours earlier, but at that moment, it was a shocking change in plans, especially for my wife. While she had intellectually understood that the C-section was a possible outcome, she hadn't emotionally prepared for anything other than a "natural" birth.

The whole mood shifted once the doctors decided to perform the surgery, and a rush of activity kicked off. A seemingly unending parade of new doctors and nurses came into the room—some giving new information, others physically preparing Erin for the C-section. It felt like a whirlwind, with neither of us having time to process what was happening. My wife was crying, and my stress level was rising by the minute. Eventually, I told the doctor, "Unless you tell me this is an emergency, we're going to need ten minutes." Without that intervention, the surgery parade would have continued.

The point of sharing that story is that what happened at several moments in the process differed from what my wife and I had imagined. So, while it may be helpful to have a birth plan that outlines your preferences and helps you have a conversation with the doctor, it pays to hold that plan lightly and to discuss with your partner what you'd want to do if Plan A doesn't work out.

A NOTE ON CESAREAN BIRTHS

The U.S. CDC indicates that almost 32% of births in 2018

were by cesarean section,[5] so it's not uncommon. And while some would claim that doctors over-medicalize births, there are several medical reasons for doing a C-section. According to the American College of Obstetricians and Gynecologists, these include the failure of labor to progress, concerns for the baby, like a pinched umbilical cord or abnormal heart rate, and pre-existing medical conditions of the mother that increase risk.[6]

Despite how common C-sections are, switching from a "natural" birth to a surgical birth may feel to your wife like a failure or a deviation from "normal"—or at least that's how my wife felt. As you prepare for your dad role in the birth process, it's worth thinking about supporting the emotional journey in addition to the physical one.

BE READY FOR ACTION

This funny bit from Sebastian Maniscalco's *Stay Hungry* comedy special is instructive:

> We went to the delivery room. I thought this thing was going to be packed in the delivery room. Sold out. Doctors, nurses, specialists, some interns... Nothing! It's me, a nurse, and the doctor. And my wife starts going into labor. I go, "Wait, where's everybody?" And the doctor's like, "This is it. Grab a foot." I said, "With all the money we're paying, we don't got a foot guy?"[7]

Clarence, one of the Council of Dads members, told me a similar story. "My plan was definitely not to hold my wife's leg and literally watch my son come out, but the doctor just told me to get in the action." Don't assume you will be an audience member at the birth. You may be a supporting actor!

After the delivery, expect your partner to be out of the game. She'll also be hooked up to several tubes for the various fluids going in and out of her body. Therefore, you must be ready to do everything, including running errands, fetching water, and changing diapers. You'll also have to do some paperwork—filling out forms for the birth certificate, social security number, and local health department.

It's like a relay race. When her job is done, you've got to grab the baton.

(By the way, doing the paperwork also gives you a lot of power over the kid's name. My friend's father, for example, decided on a different name for their kid while his wife was still out of it. I'm not saying you should do that—see the later section on how not to get divorced—but it's possible.)

DON'T TANK YOUR MARRIAGE

There's a period before and after delivery when your wife will not be able to eat. Hence, it might irreparably harm your marriage to come into the delivery or recovery room with food that looks or smells good.

I know from first-hand experience. As mentioned in the previous chapter, I went home right after Zola was born to get the right supplies for the hospital stay. To get back to the hospital as quickly as possible, I went for fast food—a slice of pepperoni pizza from our neighborhood shop.

Huge mistake. As soon as I walked into the recovery room, my wife got a whiff of the pizza and was pissed. I haven't heard the end of it to this day. Erin's memory of that moment: "I wanted to slam your face into the pizza box for bringing that smell into the room when you knew that I couldn't have any."

You've been warned.

LEVERAGE THE NURSES

"The nurses are the best-trained babysitters you'll ever get. And they're free."

That's advice from Dan, one of the Council members. He's referring to the fact that when you're at the hospital, the nurses will take your kid when you need it. Whereas you won't know what the hell you're doing, the nurses have years of study and experience with babies. That's a gift from Heaven when you're struggling, can't get to sleep, or need a break.

You won't have this high-quality support when you go home, so take advantage of it.

DON'T PANIC IF YOUR KID LOSES WEIGHT

It's natural for your kid to lose some of their birth weight. The doctors will let you know if there's an issue. Regardless, the answer to weight problems is almost always simple—more food.

If you have to give more food to your kid, it'll likely be in the form of formula or breast milk mixed with formula. And while breast milk is generally seen as better because it helps build the baby's immune system, formula is unlikely to cause an issue with breastfeeding.

As Emily Oster writes in *Cribsheet*, "[T]o the extent that we know anything, we know there's no reason to think a short period of supplementing with formula should impact breastfeeding success (if that is your goal) in the long run."[8] Oster also shares that there is little risk of nipple confusion from using the bottle—or even a pacifier. "Despite the warnings, there is simply no evidence that the use of pacifiers impacts breastfeeding success."[9]

If your wife is anything like mine, she may already have a strong opinion about choosing between breast milk and formula. It's quite the hot topic in the mommy wars, so expect that she will have formed a clear preference and plan for breastfeeding (or not). More importantly, "providing enough sustenance for the kid" may be a central part of her identity as a mom. As such, your kid losing too much weight or having to supplement with formula—especially if the weight loss is

related to issues with breastfeeding—may be an emotional hit to that identity.

So, if you face this challenge, don't assume it is only a technical issue to be solved. Tread carefully and empathetically. And maybe do whatever your wife wants.

SIDEBAR: HOW TO CHANGE A DIAPER

Changing a diaper for the first time can be a little nerve-wracking. After all, it's a complex procedure of taking off and putting underwear on a human being.

Since your wife is pregnant, you've already proven that you can take off the underwear of another human being, but if you're still uncertain, here's a step-by-step guide to help you.

STEP 1

Man the f- up and just change the diaper.

STEP 2

Whisper to yourself, "I'm the greatest father of all time."

CRUSHING IT
BACK AT HOME

It's hard to describe,
but the kid becomes
all-consuming in ways
I would never have
expected.

—

Clarence

This chapter is about what to expect when you first come home from the hospital with your newborn.

Hint: It's probably going to be a train wreck.

But you got this.

BE READY FOR ACTION (PART II)

When you get home, your wife will still be physically limited. If she has a C-section, the recovery time is even longer. For example, she may be unable to walk up and down stairs often.

Irrespective of the birth method, your wife will be going through hormonal changes and, potentially, postpartum depression (see below). So think about how you'll work with and around all of that.

A NOTE ON POSTPARTUM DEPRESSION

This is a big topic—way more can be said about it than there is space here. The main thing to know is that postpartum depression is common. According to the U.S. Centers for Disease Control and Prevention (CDC), 1 in 8 women experience symptoms,[10] as do some men.[11] The symptoms of postpartum depression may include crying more often than usual, feeling angry, feeling distant from the baby, doubting your ability to care for the baby, feeling overly anxious, and thinking about hurting yourself or the baby.[12]

Your wife's doctor will check for postpartum depression during her follow-up visits, but you can also be on the lookout for signs of depression.

What can you do about it?

The thrust of the advice from experts is to give your wife (and yourself) opportunities to take a break, especially sleep breaks.[13] That means being proactive about childcare and household chores.

In other words, you need to be ready to get in the game.

DON'T PANIC!

In my experience, more than half of the success formula in parenting a newborn is simple: Don't panic.

Instead, be a problem solver.

Yes, a crying baby is stressful. But it's easier to deal with if you take your time and progress through a checklist like this:

1. Wait a second to see if the problem is temporary. Sometimes, the kid will stop crying without you doing anything. If not...

2. Do a smell test or visual inspection for poop. If not...

3. When was the last time the kid ate? Just like you sometimes get hungry before your appointed meal time, your kid will not be on a rigid schedule. "It's only been two hours since they last ate" is faulty logic. Your kid will go through periods of more frequent eating and growing. Just go with it. If it's not meal time...

4. Hold them for a while. If that doesn't work...

5. Hold them while moving around.

If none of that works, ride it out.

The key is that as you work through that process, you can focus on what you can do about the problem. That feeling of agency helps keep the stress away. When we're active, things are more manageable. When we're lost in the issue at hand, things are worse.

I wish I had known
that organizing sleep
for your family is
probably the single
hardest thing about
having a kid.

———

Benjamin

THE SHITSHOW OF GETTING THE BABY'S SLEEP RIGHT

Finding the right sleep situation is an experimental process. Things that work for other parents might not work for you, and no device or technique is 100% effective, no matter what the advertising says. So, keep trying stuff—different rooms, room temperatures, and sounds. You'll figure it out as long as you keep problem-solving.

Some other ideas:

SET A BEDTIME ON DAY 1

My sister-in-law, Elizabeth, gave us the best advice we received as new parents. My wife and I had a disastrous first night home from the hospital. We got no sleep and couldn't figure out what we were doing wrong in getting Zola to sleep. Elizabeth's advice was to start the baby on a schedule immediately—and that night, we instituted a 7 p.m. bedtime.

Don't get me wrong—this was not a magic solution, and Zola did not automatically go to sleep right at 7 p.m. But having a bedtime for our kid helped us create a consistent routine. Virtually every article or book about baby sleep will cite consistency as a critical factor in helping them eventually sleep through the night.

That said, the primary benefit of implementing a bedtime for the baby was really for us as parents. It provided structure to the day. Zola's bedtime provided a finish line to the day—when I knew I would be able to have a glass of scotch and relax. It was the first step in feeling like I had things under control.

Also, the scotch was exquisite.

DON'T READ TO YOUR KIDS AT BEDTIME

One night, we had friends over for dinner and drinks. When it was time for the kids to go to bed, I went upstairs to start the bath and set out their daily medicine. About ten minutes later, I returned to the dinner party.

My friend asked about the kids' bedtime routine, "Wait—is that it?"

I was puzzled by his question. "What else would there be?" He then described how his other friends have extended bedtime routines, sometimes stretching for almost an hour.

It was the first time I recognized that we had stumbled into a practice early in our parenting that continues to help us today. Specifically, all of the activities we do to wind down the day, including reading books, happen *before* the bedtime routine starts. Bedtime was only ever about getting clean and putting on pajamas.

We established that practice to create a bright line for the kids between their time with us and when they were expected to be in their bedrooms. The kids know they can stay awake for as long as they want, but they no longer have a right to talk to us or to spread their noise throughout the house.

As a result, while the kids might still ask if they can come downstairs for one more hug, we are never stuck in their bedroom based on requests to read one more book or to tell a story. And they readily accept statements like, "Close your door if you will be making noise" and "I'm not having any more conversation with you tonight because it's past bedtime."

Our early practices set the foundation for those expectations. The lesson for you is to think now about what household routines you want to implement. Your kids only see one example—whatever you choose to do will seem normal to them. It's easier to set a norm before they realize it than to break a norm once it is established.

"SLEEP WHEN YOUR KID IS SLEEPING" IS B.S.

"Sleep when your kid is sleeping" is standard advice for new parents. But while the sentiment is helpful, there's no way

you could follow your kid's sleep schedule—because you're an adult.

The better advice is to take a *break* when your kid is sleeping. That break may be a nap, but it could be taking a walk, calling a friend, exercising, playing video games, or whatever you do to remain a sane human being.

The major caution is that you'll need to manage your sleep schedule. For example, you should monitor your caffeine intake since having too much can prevent you from falling asleep when you desperately need it. And, if you mess around in the evening instead of going to sleep, you'll pay more dearly after you have kids than ever before. It's kind of like how tired you are at work the day after staying up to watch a movie... but it's five times worse. You can count on your sleep being less-than-awesome with a newborn, but don't kick yourself in the groin by wasting time when you could be asleep.

However, if your newborn causes you to have a chaotic sleep schedule, one upside is that you may have time to get through a lot of content you've wanted to watch, read, and listen to. I recently checked out my Netflix viewing activity from when my first kid was a newborn. In just the first six weeks of her life, I watched 15 movies, several seasons of *The West Wing*, and every episode of *The League*. And I'm sure half of that was between 12 and 3 a.m. while rocking Zola back to sleep.

PAUSE

Your kid needs to *learn* how to sleep through the night, and one way to do that is to not be on top of every noise during the night. In the book *Bringing Up Bébé*, Pamela Druckerman recommends the French method of pausing before engaging your kid:

Another reason for pausing is that babies wake up between their sleep cycles, which last about two hours. It's normal for them to cry a bit when they're first learning to connect these cycles. If a parent automatically interprets this cry as a demand for food or a sign of distress and rushes in to soothe the baby, the baby will have a hard time learning to connect the cycles on his own. That is, he'll need an adult to come in and soothe him back to sleep at the end of each cycle.[14]

So when you hear your kid making noise, wait five or ten minutes before waking them up. You might also find it helpful to set a timer for yourself since it's easy to lose track of time—and lose your willpower—if you only focus on the fact that your kid is crying.

A little crying will not hurt your kid, even if you eventually use the "cry it out" method of sleep training. From Emily Oster's *Cribsheet*: "There is no evidence of long- or short-term harm to infants; if anything, there may be some evidence of short-term benefits."[15]

Relax. Your kid will be okay.

SIDEBAR: BATHTIME

If you're over 30, you've (hopefully) washed yourself over 10,000 times. Washing the baby is essentially the same thing.

Don't let people tell you it's more complicated. Yeah, there are some nuances around the umbilical cord and a circumcised penis—they'll explain it to you in the hospital. And there are nooks and crannies that you take for granted in your bathing—I always forget about cleaning well behind my kid's ears—but giving a bath is simply washing human skin. You got this.

Your kid may cry if they don't like the water, but they're fine unless it's scalding hot. In any case, the bath only takes a couple of minutes.

Finally, don't drop a slippery kid. But you already knew that.

	BATHING YOURSELF	BATHING A BABY
Run the water	✓	✓
…until the water is hot	✓	✕
Get soapy	✓	✓
Scrub hard	✓	✕
Get up in those crevices	✓	✓
Relax and let your mind wander	✓	✕
Don't slip and bust your ass on the bathroom floor	✓	✓
Towel off, moisturize	✓	✓
Walk around naked, like you own the place	✓	**why not?**

TAKING PARENTAL LEAVE

How much parental leave to take is a personal choice, and everyone's in a different situation.

One reason to take as much leave as possible is that you won't get it back—either with your kid or employer—if you don't. And even if you don't think you need the leave, your partner needs you in those first few weeks. It's for her sake more than anything.

That said, it's possible to have too many cooks in the kitchen. For example, if a grandparent is coming to stay for an extended time, you will find situations where three adults are standing around and staring at one kid. That's more than you need. It might be more beneficial to save some of your leave for a few months after grandma returns home or when your partner transitions back to work.

AVOIDING DIVORCE BY WEEK 3

I wish I had known how hard it is on the mom those first few months—breastfeeding, pumping every 3 hours throughout the night, wondering what was happening to her job while she was away, not being able to look or dress or feel like herself for weeks.

Albert

If your kids are crying, you can wait. But if your wife is complaining, you need to address that right away.

—

Dan

There are plenty of single parents out there. Bless them—that's a ton of work. If you have a partner in the journey, the last thing you want to do is fuck it up and have to take care of your kid by yourself. There's a reason one of the dads in the Council told me that "an engagement ring" was the single best purchase for making fatherhood easier.

The problem for many of us is that the parenting workload can easily make our marriage a lower priority for our time and attention, which can lead to strain. This chapter will help you avoid that.

RELAX

For your sanity, remember these facts.

- Your newborn can be left alone for a few minutes (obviously, in a safe spot).

- Your newborn can't move on their own.

- Crying for a few minutes won't scar them.

- You don't need to change the diaper the second the yellow strip turns blue.

You're a human being. Enjoy a legit shower. Finish your coffee. Take a deuce with the privacy of a closed bathroom door. If you let your kid take those joys away from you, you're screwed.

More importantly, when you're relaxed, your kid will be more relaxed, and your interactions with your wife will be more relaxed. This is Step A of the divorce avoidance plan.

Part of staying relaxed is recognizing some parenting math. "About three hours since the last time the kid ate" is functionally the same as "exactly three hours since the last time the kid ate." Your kid doesn't own a watch. They won't know the difference. Similarly, About 4 oz of milk is functionally equivalent to precisely 4 oz. Bedtime at 7:15 p.m. is the same as bedtime at 7:00 p.m. You get the point.

Stressing about getting those things exactly right doesn't help the kid and adds stress to *your* life.

KEEP YOUR FRIGGIN' OPINIONS TO YOURSELF

Of course, if your partner cares about those slight differences and tries to parent with military precision, I wouldn't try to convince her that the distinctions don't matter. Let her figure it out in her own time.

What you may need to master, however, is the discipline to walk away from potential conflicts, especially if the conflict might lead you to say anything that could come off as judgmental of her parenting. Trust me on this one. Don't get fired.

PHRASES TO KEEP YOUR MARRIAGE STRONG WHILE PARENTING

1. "Yes."

2. "I'm sure you're right about this."

3. "Sure—let's try and see how it works."

4. "That's totally reasonable."

5. "Your mom is a great help. I'm happy for her to stay for as long as it's helpful for you."

6. "I'm not sure. What do you think?"

7. "I'll be right there. I'm in here doing [something that's plausibly for the baby]."

8. "Yes, dear."

PRO TIP: START PRACTICING NOW.

CONSIDER PRE-PLANNED RESPONSES

Pre-planned responses (PPRs) are guidelines for how you and your partner will get stuff done. They create clear responsibilities and help you avoid conflict. Some areas where you may find this concept relevant:

FEEDING

My wife Erin and I had a recurring conflict about me giving a bottle of breast milk to Zola when my wife was out of the house, and it followed almost the exact same pattern.

Zola would start crying. I would check how long it had been since her last meal, and if enough time had passed, I would feed her. Shortly thereafter, Erin would get home and express her frustration that I had not waited for her arrival so that she could breastfeed the kid.

While out, Erin would be thinking, "I want to relieve myself of this milk when I get home (so everything should go according to that unexpressed plan)." At home, I would be thinking, "Yeah, but the kid's crying *right now* (and all I care about is getting the crying to stop)."

Because it was a frequent flashpoint, we eventually developed PPRs to prevent the argument.

The PPR protocol was this:

1. If you're out and would prefer that I wait to feed the kid, then you need to give a precise arrival time and be home exactly at that time.

2. If there's no milk ready, then formula is fine.

3. Whatever happens, we won't make the kid wait more than seven minutes for food.

4. Trust the parent in charge to make the best decision. There's no second-guessing, especially if you're not

there. (This is a general rule in our house across all dimensions of parenting.)

Equipped with those PPRs, my wife might be disappointed that she couldn't breastfeed (and thus had to pump), but it reduced the conflict between us because there was a framework for the decision, and the framework acknowledged both of our perspectives.

All that said, this conversation is still difficult—mostly because Mom is producing the milk and you. ain't. doin'. shit. (Not that my wife said it exactly that way to me.) I wouldn't assume that you can completely remove the conflict. My suggestion is to (a) make that imbalance explicit and (b) focus on the fact that the cost of Mom's ability to have some freedom is letting Dad be in charge.

CHANGING DIAPERS

No one likes to change diapers. It's literally a shitty job.

When we knew Zola needed a diaper change, my wife and I would often debate who should do it. But the debates were just a cover for the fact that both of us were trying to shirk the task.

Adopting a PPR was useful in breaking the logjam. Ours was: "If you smell poop, you must investigate; if you see poop, you must change." No debate necessary.

(My wife developed a very narrow and temporary loss of smell as it relates to our youngest kid. She could smell every time I passed gas, but when the baby pooped, she'd somehow become nose-blind. Yes, it's very curious.)

NIGHTTIME

Like with the diapers, you and your partner will be peeved about getting up in the dead of night to handle the kid. When Zola would cry, my wife and I would debate who should get up—but the evening debates were fraught with extreme fatigue and value-laden notions about responsibility and who's putting in what amount of effort. In reality, we both just wanted to stay in bed and sleep more.

To handle this scenario more productively, our PPR was, "If it's been three hours since the kid last ate, Mom will go. If it's been less than that, Dad will."

Across each of these areas, the specifics of the rules you and your partner develop will matter less than the process of understanding each others' perspectives and the commitment to avoid conflict when you're not at your best. Preventing conflict that comes from being stressed is far easier than cleaning up after a marital blowout (or a diaper blowout that comes while you're debating who does the change!).

GET FREEDOM BY LEARNING HOW TO MANAGE

WITH JUST ONE PARENT AT A TIME

One of the more challenging parts of parenting is that it's an always-on job—and one of the few jobs where the weekends are more brutal than the weekdays. Gary, one of the Council members, said: "This sounds ignorant, but I didn't know how much of a full-on commitment having kids was and how my life would instantly derail into having much less control over everything."

The all-consuming nature of parenting is even harder for those of us who are introverts. If I'm around the kids, there is always someone talking to me! Hence, for me, a critical part of making parenting manageable is finding regular *alone, I'm-not-responsible time*. It makes all the difference.

You and your partner may value this kind of time as well. It's no fun and no good for the relationship for you to look over each other's shoulders constantly, and it's great to take a nap with no guilt or worry. Achieving those goals, however, requires you and your partner to feel comfortable being in charge alone and letting the other person be in charge alone. In my experience, this is an emotional calculation more than anything, and it just takes time. You can start down that path early by letting yourself take mini-breaks from parenting and increasing those to several hours away.

It'll be clutch. Trust me on this.

Moreover, operating with man-on-man coverage becomes even more critical when both parents are back at work. My research with working parents suggests that the family system only works if each person can confidently tag out when needed.

PLAY RELATIONSHIP OFFENSE

The previous sections in this chapter have been about avoiding conflict—i.e., preventing damage to your relationship with your partner. However, you should also take proactive steps to keep your relationship strong. Consider the following:

SCHEDULE A RELATIONSHIP CHECK-IN

After reading to this point in the book, it should be obvious that your life will be different after you have kids. However, what you won't know until you've experienced parenting firsthand is how exactly things will be different or how you and your partner will feel about it.

Consider proposing to your partner that you schedule time now for a few months after the birth to check how your marriage and parenting partnership is going. You might discuss questions like:

- How is it going for you?

- What's not going well? What adjustments should we make?

- How is our household system working? Are we allocating chores efficiently and equitably?

- How are we spending money now? Do we need to make adjustments?

Asking those questions of each other can help you identify what changes you need.

DO THE SAME RELATIONSHIP STUFF YOU DO NOW

Perhaps the key to maintaining the quality of your relationship is not abandoning all of the things you do right now—before kids—to keep it strong.

Do you hang out with friends? Keep doing it. You can take a newborn to a bar—your kid will likely sleep through it anyway.

Do you have a regular date night? Keep doing that.

Do you do a catch-up at the end of each day? You guessed it, keep doing it.

One of the Council members, Benjamin, advises: "Figure out how you can have vacations, or just extended time, alone without your kid."

You already know what it takes to make your relationship strong. It becomes more challenging after you have kids, but it's not a fundamentally different equation.

KEEPING YOUR KID ALIVE AND HEALTHY

I wish I had known how my dreams of raising a child genius would be replaced by just wanting happy and healthy kids, especially after seeing how others have struggled even to have kids.

———

Gary

As I prepared to become a father, I thought my primary task was protection—keeping the kid healthy and alive. Naturally, I wondered, "What's everything that could go wrong?" Fortunately, my research and subsequent experience as a father have led me to a basic conclusion: Kids are designed to survive and thrive.

The reason to start there is that parenting is far more stressful and far less enjoyable if you are worried about extremely low-likelihood events that you have no control over anyway.

But even though the risk is very low, there are areas in which you can lower the potential for harm to your kid. Read below.

PHYSICAL INJURIES AND CHILDPROOFING

Among the bad things that could happen is sudden infant death (SIDS), which usually occurs when a baby who does not have the muscle strength to turn over has obstructed breathing. SIDS is very rare (0.04% of kids[16]), but the prevention is straightforward. The American Academy of Pediatrics provides several recommendations, most of which are about good sleep hygiene, including back sleeping, having a firm sleep surface, and keeping the sleeping area uncluttered.[17]

Other than suffocation, the leading sources of injury for young kids are, in order, motor vehicle accidents, drowning, burns, and poisoning.[18]

So yeah, if you care about your kid, the first step is to drive more carefully. For everything else, this is what childproofing your house is for.

The good news is that you don't need to worry about serious childproofing immediately, as your kid won't be able to move. But when you get to that stage, most of the steps will come down to:

· Restricting access to household cleaners and chemicals, medicines, sharp objects, firearms, and pools

· Preventing your kid from falling out of windows, off of balconies, and down a flight of stairs

· Watching your kid at all times in the bath

· Having working fire and carbon monoxide alarms

Once you're ready to start childproofing, there are many resources to guide you, including from the National Safety Council.[19] Fortunately, the work to get it all done can be accomplished with a quick trip to the hardware store and an afternoon of man time. You got this.

EMOTIONAL INJURIES

You should also care about preventing traumatic experiences for your kid that make them feel less safe, stable, and able to bond with others.[20] Some examples of these adverse experiences include witnessing violence, experiencing abuse or neglect, being in a household with substance abuse or mental health challenges, and extended separation from parents. If you ever needed a reason to stay out of prison, this is just one more. These traumatic experiences can negatively impact your kids' mental and emotional development, which can harm their long-term prospects.

Luckily, the solution is simple: Pay attention to your kid and re-read the chapter on "Avoiding Divorce by Week 3." And if you're doing crimes, just don't let the police catch you.

GOING BACK
TO WORK

I wish I had known the sheer time commitment to doing it right. You're picking up a 20+ hours/week volunteer commitment for a decade or two.

———

Matt

Maternity and paternity leave aren't trips to the beach. Beyond caring for a newborn all day, parental leave can be especially tough due to the lack of regular adult interaction. If you're returning to work first, be mindful of what your partner is going through. This starts with asking, "How is it going?" when you arrive home.

You should also arrange your workday so that you can arrive home on time. Much like setting a clear bedtime gives you a finish line for the day, your partner may use your arrival as her mental marker (e.g., "I just need to make it until 5:45 p.m.").

Finally, create a transition routine that you can do before you get home so that you're mentally ready to take over almost immediately when you step in the door. Saying, "Give me 10 minutes; I just need a little me time," will generate needless conflict.

In fact, you might lose your life if you say that.

CONSIDER REFRAMING HOW WORK FITS IN YOUR LIFE

Among the many changes after you have kids, you should be ready to think about work through a different lens.

A college friend, a tax lawyer, told me he was worried about not finding much meaning in his work. Tax law is not the kind of thing that drives most people wild. That was before had kids.

After having kids, however, his need to find meaning at work decreased. Instead, work became a vehicle to meet his responsibilities to what provided even more meaning—

family. After changing his approach, he only needed work to be "good enough" because he was fulfilled in other areas of his life. A decade later, he's still a tax lawyer.

Todd, a senior executive at the company where I used to work, told me after he found out I was expecting my first kid, "Forget about being exceptional (the highest performance rating) next year." Regardless of the situation, Todd's prediction was almost surely going to be correct since my performance ratings always leaned more toward "this guy still works here?" than "exceptional." But his point was that when you have a kid, you will be too exhausted to perform at your best. You can put in a good effort, but it's worth getting comfortable with the fact that your effort won't be at your peak.

PROACTIVELY MANAGE YOUR ENERGY

If you think you'll be able to do eight hours of effective work when you're experiencing repeated nights of interrupted sleep, you're delusional. Coffee might not even provide the jolt of energy you need.

When you return to work, part of taking a different approach entails paying attention to how your energy flows during the day and making your calendar accommodate it. For example, it was helpful for me to institute a calendar block for 1-2 p.m. in case I needed a nap—and I almost always *crushed* the nap room.

I also avoided scheduling the last hour of the day since my energy would typically wane. Some days, I even had to take a power nap at 4:30 p.m. to ensure I had enough energy to drive home without crashing my car.

Yeah, it can get that bad.

SEX

"

R

On our business school class survey…

On the question "Number of times you have sex per month," why wasn't "fewer than 1 time" an option?

Haha. My reaction was: "Who has the energy for more than 1 time per week?"

You spelled "month" wrong

Haha. Yeah, you can forget about it for a while.

You just have to wait until your partner says she's interested, and that may not come right after the doctor-recommended six-week recovery period.

And even then, the sex may not get back to "normal" frequency and quality for up to a year.[21] Given the hormone changes and physical trauma of birth, there could be a lot of stuff going on *down there*. And you both might be tired and just not into it.

Dude, handle your own business.

I wish there were a better story to tell you, but there's none.

THE
EMOTIONAL
SIDE OF
FATHERHOOD

I wish I had known how quickly kids would expose my faults and shortcomings. Very effective.

———

Mike

If you want a good description of fatherhood, watch Mike Birbiglia's hilarious comedy special, *The New One*. He very aptly describes the joys and absurdities of the endeavor. The line from the special that stuck out to me most was Mike's brother's statement on fatherhood: "You can't know what it's like to have a kid until you have a kid." That's so true. There are as many reactions to fatherhood as there are people, and you won't know what yours will be until you're knee-deep in it.

The fact that I included sections with the headlines RELAX and DON'T PANIC is a testament to how important managing your emotional experience of fatherhood is to your success. Let's explore those emotions in a bit more detail.

DURING THE PREGNANCY

If you haven't already noticed, almost no one will ask you how you're doing during the pregnancy—they're only concerned about mom. Get used to it. While you will see a lot of content on what mom is facing—the hormonal changes, the mood swings, the cravings—there's very little open discussion of what dads experience.

According to *The Expectant Father*, "The reality is that men's emotional response to pregnancy is no less varied than women's; expectant fathers feel everything from relief to denial, fear to frustration, anger to joy."[22]

Your feelings might run the gamut of:

- Excitement that you'll be a dad

- Uncertainty about what the hell you should be doing

- Worrying about whether you'll be good at it

- Coach Prime-level swagger that comes with proving your potency

- Jealousy that you can't do more to support the kid's development

- Resentment that your wife pays less attention to you

- Frustration that you're having less sex

- Anxiety as the due date approaches

- A fierce protective streak

...and more.

Those thoughts and emotions are legit, and many dads experience them. As with anything, exploring your feelings, talking to others about them, or doing whatever you do to keep things moving is a good idea. Don't overlook your mental health process.

For some, your wife may be a good outlet for that conversation, but for others, your wife might not be ready to hear your angst when she's experiencing morning sickness, swollen feet, and the inability to walk down the street. You might need to carry some of your emotions without her or look to others for support.

BONDING WITH YOUR KID

Bonding comes differently for every dad. For some, there's an instant love-at-first-sight bond with their kids. For others, it takes a little time. In his excellent book *Home Game*, Michael Lewis writes, "Maternal love may be instinctive, but paternal love is learned behavior."[23] Rick, one of the Council members, said, "[I]t's ok not to feel an instantaneous bond with your child, especially if they're challenging (e.g., colic). The bond forms and changes over time." On *The Ezra Klein*

Show podcast, Mike Birbiglia described not feeling a strong bond with his daughter until she was more verbal and they could communicate with words.[24]

In *Dad is Fat*, Jim Gaffigan wrote of his experience, "I'm not surprised by how much I love my children. I'm relieved."[25]

Regardless of your initial feelings, there are many ways to strengthen your attachment to your kid—talking to them, cuddling, and playing games. All that's important. In the book *The New Father*, Armin Brott describes this work as investing in your kid and your relationship with them, even if they can't communicate their thanks to you. It's an article of faith that the investment will pay off.[26]

In the meantime, the cuddles are amazing. They'll help.

MANAGING YOUR OWN SHIT

Michael Lewis reported that fatherhood "perverted" his attitude toward risk. An example:

> Not long after our first child was born, but well before September 11, 2001, I began to experience a mild fear of flying. There was a time in my life when I could, fairly blithely, hop out of an airplane with a parachute on my back; now I can't get onto an airplane without melodramatic feelings of doom.[27]

I personally had an irrational fear that I would get mugged while putting my kids in their car seats because my back was turned for 20 seconds. I was also afraid that I would fall down the steps while carrying them and cause a traumatic brain injury. So don't be surprised if you have your own version of these fears.

Here's the thing: the time, effort, and emotions of parenting come *on top of* whatever else you have going on right now. If you're an anxious person, being a father might not help. If you're starting with a lot of stress, there's nowhere to go but into the red zone. My advice is that if you're not currently in a good place mentally or emotionally, find whatever resources you need to help you get there.

If you are in a good place and have a set of routines that keep you emotionally healthy, make sure you keep doing them after the kid comes.

TAKING BREAKS

Shortly after Big Time was born, my wife took both kids to Texas to visit her parents. Since she was on maternity leave and I had gone back to work, I stayed at home. When I imagined the week, I thought it would be an excellent opportunity to get to bed early and beat down my sleep deficit.

That's the exact opposite of what happened. I stayed at work a little later each day because I wasn't on a strict deadline for relieving the nanny. Instead of going home, I went to happy hour or went shopping. Did I need a new suit or a new watch? No. But that's what happens when you can casually stroll in the mall. Instead of getting to sleep early, I ate dinner late and watched movies without the fear that one of the kids would wake me up at 6:00 a.m. the next day.

Mostly, I enjoyed the peace. It was glorious. It turns out that what I needed more than sleep was liberty.

At the start of this book, I joked that fatherhood is like a minimum-security prison. That analogy came from a conversation with my father. He once told me, as an adult, "Raising kids was great, but I really value the freedom to do what I want now."

I replied, "Geez, you say it like you were in prison."

After pausing to consider, he said, "Well, yeah, something like that."

If parenting is like prison, taking breaks is your furlough. If you can get an hour, day, or weekend of freedom, take it. The only gifts my wife and I give each other for our birthdays, Mother's Day, and Father's Day is the day off from childcare.

The break is worth way more than anything money could buy.

CLOSING
THOUGHTS

"

I wish I had known that kids figure out most of what they learn on their own—without your help.

———

Mark

'll end this book where it started. The core thesis of this book is that you have all the skills you need to succeed. If you're focused on being "good enough," on problem-solving rather than panicking, and on keeping your wife happy, you'll be good to go.

I wish you luck as you take on this next journey.

And when things get tough, remember this: Your dad wasn't that good, and you turned out just fine!

APPENDIX

A QUICK REQUEST

Did you enjoy this book? Please leave a review on Amazon or wherever you purchased this book! Every review helps!

Even better, buy a copy for a dude who is expecting. This is the only way my kids will ever go to college without debt.

Thanks again for reading!

ABOUT THE AUTHOR

Charles Moore is the CEO of Thrive Street Advisors and a trusted executive coach and strategy consultant to nonprofit, for-profit, and government leaders. Charles holds a bachelor's degree from Harvard and a master's degree in business and education from Stanford.

None of that official stuff matters for this book, however. The real story is that Charles is the father of two kids, Zola (7) and Big Time (5), and the husband of Erin (age undisclosed). They live in Washington, D.C.

He's proven time and again that he's definitely the world's okayest dad and barely keeping things together.

ACKNOWLEDGMENTS

A book is always a group effort. I'd like to thank The Distinguished Council of Dads—Shaka, Albert, Ken, Matt, Mike, Dan, Dave, Clarence, Mark, Mason, Rick, Gary, Andrew, Benjamin, and Ian—for contributing their perspectives.

Thanks to Gerard and Bergie for their support in the writing process, namely for joking around and inspiring the content. Thanks to Paul, Jon, Ian, Clarence, Albert, and Gellis for reading early drafts and providing encouragement and feedback. Kammy Wood helped with editing, though, of course, any mistakes are all mine.

Finally, thank you for reading and for propagating the species.

ENDNOTES

1   Emily Oster, *Expecting Better: Why the Conventional Pregnancy Wisdom Is Wrong—and What You Really Need to Know* (New York: Penguin Publishing Group, 2014), e-book, 194.

2   Matthew Rae, Cynthia Cox, and Hanna Dingel, "Health costs associated with pregnancy, childbirth, and postpartum care," Peterson Kaiser Family Foundation Health System Tracker, 13 July 2022, https://www.healthsystemtracker.org/brief/health-costs-associated-with-pregnancy-childbirth-and-postpartum-care/.

3   Mark Lino, et al., "Expenditures on Children by Families, 2015," U.S. Department of Agriculture, Center for Nutrition Policy and Promotion, January 2017, https://fns-prod.azureedge.us/sites/default/files/resource-files/crc2015-march2017.pdf.

4   Ibid.

5   Joyce A. Martin, et al., "Births: Final data for 2018," National Vital Statistics Reports, 27 Nov 2019, https://www.cdc.gov/nchs/data/nvsr/nvsr68/nvsr68_13-508.pdf.

6   American College of Obstetricians and Gynecologists, "Cesarean Birth," May 2022, Accessed Aug 1, 2020, https://www.acog.org/patient-resources/faqs/labor-delivery-and-postpartum-care/cesarean-birth.

7   *Sebastian Maniscalco: Stay Hungry,* Directed by Rik Reinholdtsen, Netflix Studios, 2019.

8   Emily Oster, *Cribsheet: A Data-Driven Guide to Better, More Relaxed Parenting, from Birth to Preschool* (New York: Penguin, 2019), e-book, 21.

9   Ibid, 96.

10   Brenda Bauman, et al., "Postpartum Depressive Symptoms and Provider Discussions About Perinatal

Depression — United States, 2018," US Department of Health and Human Services, Centers for Disease Control and Prevention, 15 May 2020, https://www.cdc.gov/mmwr/volumes/69/wr/pdfs/mm6919a2-H.pdf.

11 Cleveland Clinic, "Yes, Postpartum Depression in Men Is Very Real," July 11, 2024, health.clevelandclinic.org/yes-postpartum-depression-in-men-is-very-real.

12 Centers for Disease Control and Prevention, "Symptoms of Depression Among Women," 15 May 2024, www.cdc.gov/reproductive-health/depression/index.html.

13 Postpartum Support International, "Help for Partners and Families," accessed Oct. 28, 2024, https://www.postpartum.net/get-help/family/.

14 Pamela Druckerman, *Bringing up Bébé: One American Mother Discovers the Wisdom of French Parenting* (New York: Penguin, 2012), e-book, 48.

15 Oster (2019), 187.

16 Melonie Heron, "Deaths: Leading causes for 2017," National Vital Statistics Reports, 24 June 2019, https://www.cdc.gov/nchs/data/nvsr/nvsr68/nvsr68_06-508.pdf.

17 American Academy of Pediatrics Task Force on Sudden Infant Death, "SIDS and Other Sleep-Related Infant Deaths: Updated 2016 Recommendations for a Safe Infant Sleeping Environment," 1 Nov 2016, https://pediatrics.aappublications.org/content/138/5/e20162938.

18 Nagesh N. Borse, et. al, "CDC Childhood Injury Report: Patterns of Unintentional Injuries among 0 -19 Year Olds in the United States, 2000-2006," Dec 2008, Centers for Disease Control and Prevention, National Center for Injury Prevention and Control, https://stacks.cdc.gov/view/cdc/5155.

19 National Safety Council, "Childproofing Your Home," accessed July 1 2020, https://www.nsc.org/home-safety/

safety-topics/child-safety/childproofing.

20 Centers for Disease Control and Prevention, "About Adverse Childhood Experiences," 8 October 2024, www.cdc.gov/aces/about/index.html#cdc_behavioral_basics_quick-quick-facts-and-stats.

21 Oster (2019), 51.

22 Armin Brott, *The Expectant Father: The Ultimate Guide for Dads-to-Be* (New York: Abbeville Press, 2010), e-book, introduction.

23 Michael Lewis, *Home Game: An Accidental Guide to Fatherhood* (New York: W. W. Norton & Company, 2010), 75.

24 Jeff Geld (Producer), "Dadding out with Mike Birbiglia," *The Ezra Klein Show* [audio podcast], https://www.vox.com/ezra-klein-show-podcast.

25 Jim Gaffigan, *Dad is Fat* (New York: Crown Archetype, 2013), e-book, 60.

26 Armin Brott, *The New Father: A Dad's Guide to the First Year* (New York: Abbeville Press, 1997), 34.

27 Lewis, 108.